InsideOut

Elizah Peterson

InsideOut © 2022 Elizah Peterson

All rights reserved.

No part of this publication may be reproduced, stored in a retrieval system, or transmitted, in any form or by any means, electronic, mechanical, photocopying, recording or otherwise, without the prior written permission of the presenters.

Elizah Peterson asserts the moral right to be identified as author of this work.

Presentation by *BookLeaf Publishing*

Web: www.bookleafpub.com

E-mail: info@bookleafpub.com

ISBN: 9789395026383

First edition 2022

DEDICATION

I want to dedicate this book to my Children, Samson Gene and Seida Jade.

You two are the reason I breathe...Why I fight to be a better person, and would love to see you babies be loving, forgiving, honest humans.

I love you guys.

Nose.

ACKNOWLEDGEMENT

I would like to thank first and foremost: My
Family and Friends.
They have been my rock when I was a
tumbleweed in the wind.
My experiences are about many different people,
places. and choices I have made. The outcome
has not always been what was expected but, it
was maybe what I needed.
My Best friends Alesia and Dylan. You guys got
me through so much.
Pastor David and Lori, Thank you for Loving
me.
Hannah and John, I am Always thankful for
meeting you.
To The Homestead Family...You guys are my
rock.
My Beautiful Children.. Thank you for letting
me grow with you..
My Baby Daddy..You'll Always be Home.
To My Dad..You were my first Best friend. I
love you.
To My Beautiful Mother.. I Miss you..see you on
the Other side.

PREFACE

I would love to share my thoughts, experiences, failures and victories. They have made me the person that I am today. I also look forward to tomorrow's tests, to make me into my future self.

EXITWHat

Like a pitch black mansion,
The darkness and unknown are there.
With no knowledge of the Exit,
No knowledge of the entrance,
Just a wide-eyed, frightened stare.

With curiosity and exploration,
Illumination comes to the room.
Providing bits of information,
Yet, the darkness still consumes.

Who knows how many rooms are here,
The search seems tiresome and endless.
Darkened hallways, locked windows and doors,
Only bravery and persistence can mend this.

Tripping, falling, bumping and bleeding,
Obstacles around every dark corner.
Times of defeat, times of regret,
New fears lurking in every corridor.

The Exit sign is faint and far,
There are wonders beyond that door,
"Onward my mighty warrior,
There is much more to explore."

Descendent

I am but a Descendent
Of the Original
Aboriginal
Taino
Comanche
Hibara.
The Great Law of Peace.

My feet touch the land,
They feel the pain from down under.
The blood.
The tears.
The fear.

I am but a Descendent
What has changed but,
TIME?
The stars have kept their place,
The sun and moon, their rotations.
Trees still grow,
Food is still naturally produced,
The animals remember migrations.

The winds remember the names,
The faces, tribes and nations.

I hear them in it's whisper,
I feel it on my face,
What has changed but,
TIME?

I am but a Descendent
The mountains have remained in place,
The hills and valleys sleep under the stars
The seas, oceans and rivers
Know their boundaries to and fro
Seasons have kept their time,
Gatherings and feasts on one accord.

I am but a Descendent.
What has changed but,
TIME?

My Mother

I wonder where you are,
Where you went and,
If you're alone.

Do you see me?
Can you hear us?
Do you yearn to wipe our tears?

We miss you.
We need you.
We try to always remember you.

We try to take care of each other,
It's hard when we feel weak.
The sun and moon have glistened our tears,
The heartbreak forbids us to speak.

Maybe you're that star in the sky,
The rainbow that comes after the rain,
The whisper in the gentle breeze,
Saying, "I'll be seeing you again."

Sketch

I've always wanted to be an artist,
To envision, sketch and paint.
To create life on paper,
A creative way for,
Emotions to take form in a picture.

To sketch a simple picture,
In Pencil,
Black and white.
To fill the page,
To empty a cage of,
Things enraged,
People who've aged,
That we may engage,
For a moment in time
And Feel this picture of mine.

To feel what I feel,
See what I see,
To experience a glimpse of my soul.

The Window

I look out the window,
Empty streets,
Neighborhoods,
Classrooms
And Stores.
Caution tape
Encircles swings,
Jungle gyms
And slides.
Six feet
Between bodies,
Six inches
Of material
Between faces.
Smiles Disappear,
Fear is here.
Friends we hold dear
Are nowhere near.
So I look out this Window,
And imagine a time,
Where we laughed,
Hugged, Touched,
United and trusted.
Wondering "When
Will we go back?"

Pandemic Poetry

Poetry, for a time in History,
Where the world is turned upside-down.
Inside is Outside,
Uncovered is Covered and,
Confusion is all around.

Families are distant,
Friends are hesitant,
Common sense is irrelevant and,
The masses just run with it.

Hugs are obsolete,
We stand six feet apart,
A simple mask covers our face
Complete Compliance from the start.

Religion has lost faith,
Science has lost believers,
The media controls the mind and,
The government continually feeds her.

O.G.

I'm not just another kid,
Walking down the street.
Baggy pants, messy hair,
Walking to no kind of beat.

I have dreams you know,
That reach and tickle the stars.
I have seeds to plant and sow,
Dreams for now and for afar.

My dreams may look different,
From my brother's, teacher's or yours,
They may travel to different places,
To a desert or sandy shore.

Yet, only I can hear the beat to my own song,
The drums that beat,
The melody that sings,
And the words that are never wrong.

The song always plays,
Never skips a beat.
A hope the tune never changes,
And the Dance to be complete.

Free

"With age comes wisdom."
They always say.
But it seems as if I'm getting dumber,
Day by day.

Making mistakes,
Left and right,
Walking around
Eyes closed tight.

I want to be innocent,
Young and carefree,
Who cares what others think?
I just want to be me.

But, who am I?
Who is Me?
What's in the mirror?
Who is that I see?

Day by day,
Looking slightly different,
Not knowing myself,
Personality shifted.

Who are my friends?
What do they really want?
To better my life or,
Are they here to taunt?

High School life,
Brings so much grief.
When I look in the mirror,
It lies through it's teeth.

When can I leave?
To depart from this place?
To create a new mind,
A facade, a new face.

When will all those masks,
Be completely destroyed?
Forever to be gone,
And no more with be toyed?

Maybe when death comes,
And eternity is achieved,
I will be free from this life
Forever to be relieved.

Special Dayz

Those special days are over,
When you wake to the sounds of laughter,
When all you think of is candy,
When life is no more than dandy.

Those days when you can run and never stop,
When you cry because your balloon popped.
The grass seems greener, deep between your
toes,
Laughing so hard, milk sprays out your nose.

When mommy and daddy can give hugs all day ,
How they love every cute thing you say.
Feeling their voice,
Inhaling their scent,
Falling asleep,
Them knowing you are worth their every cent.

Gently they rock you,
Slower, slower, slower
Into a deep, deep sleep,
Lower, lower, lower

The world around you, is yours to explore,

You never want less because there is always
more.
The clouds can be monkeys, turtles, bees and
dragons,
They can be anything your mind can possibly
imagine.

Swinging over the top of the swing set,
Will never be impossible,
As long as I've got Daddy,
Everything is possible.

..Now there are mean people,
Who always want to fight.
Who will never understand me,
And are always quick to bite.

I don't want fast cars, boys or fights,
I don't want those cold, abandoned nights.
I don't want to lie, cheat or make mommy sad,
The things in this world seem far too bad.

I want to be that little girl,
Holding on tight to daddy's strong finger,
To run under the warm sun forever,
I don't ever want to lose her.

A New World

There in the soil,
Sleeps a tiny seed.
Thoughts of how it will one day grow and,
The places it can possibly see.

Mighty large raindrops,
Speak words of growth.
Come out little one,
Show the beauty you hold.

Sun rays pour out love,
Upon it's tiny head,
The gentle soil
Helps it ahead.

Exploring the garden,
In awe and disbelief,
Ashamed of hiding so long,
Missing this world to see.

Vibrant colors,
Burst from its petals.
Being different from the others,
Taking time for its pounding heart to settle.

Standing proud,
Growing tall and lean,
There in the soil,
Grows a beautiful dream.

I Wonder

I wonder why the stars are yellow,
Why the sun always shines so bright,
I wonder why the ocean is blue,
Why the moon only shines at night.

Why the grass is green and itchy,
Why flowers grow beautifully in spring,
Why trees only grow upward,
Why the birds fly around and sing.

I wonder how a fruit,
Comes from a tiny seed,
How it obtains it's true color,
How no fruit is exactly like another.

I wonder how a child grows and,
Is created in it's mother's body.
Every finger, toe and nose,
Is different from everybody.

I wonder how two people,
As different as can be,
Can find true love in one another,
And be together for eternity.

I wonder how a person's spirit,
Can drift so slowly away,
To return back into the earth,
For their body forever to stay.

I wonder how our minds can capture
So much information and touching memories,
How unique habits and gestures,
Can continue through a family for centuries.

I wonder how only words
Can express the way one feels,
A scary thought, a happy smile,
Words that tickle and give you the chills.

Words that could give someone life,
Bring them tears of joy and sorrow,
Words that can damage one's heart,
Bring tears and grief that follow.

Words one will always remember,
Either in a song, poem or book.
But for me, I want words of love,
That can make my heart quickly look.

I wonder..

First Love

Stranded on this deserted island,
Am I, and the whispering winds.
The melodious sounds of the glistening waters
travel through the dancing trees.
The countless number of warm, white sand,
curl underneath my toes.
Listening to the voice of the waters,
I close my eyes to seek your face.
I hear your voice through the wind in the trees.
I feel your embrace through the warmth of the
breeze
I see your eyes through the darkness of the skies.
I catch your tears and put them into the water
They disappear onto the floor of the ocean
for an eternity to pass, never to fall again.
I walk across the Island sand,
watching the sunset, such beautiful colors in the
sky
Looking down into the sand, your footprints
next to mine.

Seida Jade

She has long, dark hair
That curls at the bottom
Her eyelashes long as the nile
And freckles of course she's got 'em

Her eyes are warm and dark
Her lips are full and pink
She's got her mother's nose and
Her father's eyes I think

She is warm, caring and sweet
And loves to play outside
She loves to help and bake
And tries to outrun the tide

She loves to read books
So we sit at night and read
About Kings and Queens and castles
As she slowly slips into sleep

I look at her with an unfailing love
And thank God for entrusting me
With an angel for a Daughter
I'll do the best I can, You'll see

We Speak

We speak of your love
Of your grace and mercy
We speak of your gift
The giving of your life for me

But do we speak of your blood
Which ran thick down a tree
Full of innocence and joy
Full of salvation for me?

Or the crown of thrones
Placed harshly upon your head
The spear through your flesh
And the outpour of love that was shed

Yet there you lay
To be taken up again
Three days later
You overcame death, for my sins

Growth

Growth hurts.
A teething infant experiences pain for teeth to
grow.
A child experiences pain as their bones grow.
We also grow spiritually, emotionally and
mentally..
And we experience pain.
Letting go of what once was,
Who we were, who we've been and,
who we wanted to be.
Yet, on the other side of growth,
are beautiful things.
Knowledge, maturity, new mindsets,
new friendships and,
the opportunities and freedom to grow more.

Disbelief

Such a detailed, full world.
A clear, concise past, present and future.
I felt I knew Who I was,
Where I came from and,
What I was chasing after.

Then, things began to disappear.
Little by little, one by one.
Colors faded to nothing,
Outlines began to shift,
People, history and events,
Faded to invisibility.

Grasping, reaching for footing,
But it all just disappeared.
Everything I stood so firmly for
Everything I loved and looked forward to.
Gone.

So here I stand,
Not a thing in sight.
No color, no form, no history or future.
Hungry to know Truth.
Longing for honest information,
Desiring those colors once more.

Waiting for answers
In this empty room.

Menorah

I woke up from this Slumber.
Stumbling, bumbling, confused.
My brain so foggy,
My legs so wobbly,
Someone had lit my fuse.

I Heard "Get Out." And
A Shock went through my body,
I left everything I had ever known,
Left everyone around me.

This "Waking Up" was fierce,
The hardest thing I've been through,
I hurt, I wept, I argued and spent,
every second that I had to.

I spent my time reading,
I spent my time learning.
I spent my time Un-doing
All of the lies that forever owned me.

I was Sold Out to Religion,
Lies wrapped around my finger,
Like thornbushes around my soul,
Death so closely lingered.

I have come So very far,
Traveled this lonely road,
Met others along The Way,
That carry this heavy load.

The Load and responsibility,
Of living and sharing Torah,
This Light that illuminates The path,
A living, breathing Menorah.

To Know

Do I keep telling him?
How he makes me feel?

Waves of feelings
Like a roaring Ocean
That overtake me

Do I keep telling him?

That the sound of his voice
Makes me weak in the knees?
"Absence makes the heart grow fonder"
They say..

My insides melt
When he enters a room
focus.focus.focus.

Time, Patience, Time, Patience.

So I hold it all in
Do I keep telling him?

...Maybe Not..

His space
Tells me "No"
Yet, I want him to know
I just...

Want him to Know..

Spring

I fall for "potential"
I yield to what "could be."
I see a frozen field of snow,
I imagine the possibility of Spring.

I see hurting, broken souls,
What can I do to help them heal?
I sacrifice my soul for theirs,
But what Am I left with?

I've got this Fire in my heart,
One that cannot be smoldered.
A fountain of flowing love to give,
Yet I learn as I grow older,
So many cannot simply love,
Or receive love in return,
We're hurt, we're broken,
We're tired, we're workin',
And we never saw it first-hand.

So,
I fall for potential.
What could, or would or may be.
Because,
Sometimes winter fades,

And the sun still burns
Leaves fall away and blossoms return

28

The meeting of the Souls

When your eyes lock,
And everything stops,
To experience this moment in time.

The eyes begin to speak a language,
A language unknown to the tongue.
They stop, they gaze, they sharpen, they daze,
They sing the song they once sung.

Something so familiar, so deep,
So lost in function and color,
The outside body does not relate,
How the eyes enthrall each other.

So, look into my eyes,
We'll share a conversation,
Of life, of love,
Of things above,
Come, be my inspiration.

What If?

What if "good" comes?
What if there is Sunshine
after the rain?
What if those grey clouds
just blew away?
What if those monstrous waves
bowed down to the shore?
There's always a rainbow after the storm.

Many trees grow strong in Time.
It takes seasons and seasons,
To be able to withstand the weather.
Scorching Summer heat,
Gusty, rainy winds,
The stripping of it's beauty in fall yet,
Spring is around the corner,
New leaves, vibrant colors,
Another layer of wisdom and armor,
Stronger than the year before.
It can take years of this repetition,
To begin to produce beauty and fruit.
We respect the time, the refinement and,
Await the Beauty to withhold.

www.ingramcontent.com/pod-product-compliance
Lightning Source LLC
Chambersburg PA
CBHW060922130726
48001CB00006B/2374